To Be Canadian

BE WHO YOU WANT TO BE: FREEDOM

W9-BPR-981

TRUE NORTH

BY JOY KITA

True North is published by Beech Street Books
27 Stewart Rd. Collingwood, ON Canada L9Y 4M7

Copyright © 2018 by Beech Street Books. All rights reserved. No part of this book may be reproduced or utilized in any form or by any means without written permission from the publisher.

www.beechstreetbooks.ca

Produced by Red Line Editorial

Photographs ©: Michael Wheatley/All Canada Photos/Glow Images, cover, 1; BakerJarvis/Shutterstock Images, 4–5; PaulMcKinnon/iStockphoto, 6–7; Alexandru Nika/Shutterstock Images, 8–9; Pete Spiro/Shutterstock Images, 10–11; John R. Kennedy/Splash News/Newscom, 12–13; Shawn Goldberg/Shutterstock Images, 15; PRNewsFoto/Sustainable Forestry Initiative/AP Images, 16–17; Kevin Oke/All Canada Photos/Glow Images, 18–19

Editor: Claire Mathiowetz
Designer: Laura Polzin

Library and Archives Canada Cataloguing in Publication

Kita, Joy, author
        Be who you want to be : freedom / by Joy Kita.

 (To be Canadian)
Includes bibliographical references and index.
Issued in print and electronic formats.
ISBN 978-1-77308-137-3 (hardcover).--ISBN 978-1-77308-197-7 (softcover).--
ISBN 978-1-77308-257-8 (PDF).--ISBN 978-1-77308-296-7 (HTML)

        1. Civil rights--Canada--Juvenile literature. 2. Human rights--Canada--
Juvenile literature. 3. Canada. Canadian Charter of Rights and Freedoms--
Juvenile literature. 4. Canada--Politics and government--Juvenile literature.
I. Title.

KE4381.5.K54 2017   j342.7108'5   C2017-903930-X
KF4483.C519K54 2017   C2017-903931-8

Printed in the United States of America
Mankato, MN
August 2017

TABLE OF CONTENTS

Chapter One

WHAT IS FREEDOM?

Canadians believe in personal freedoms and rights. A right is something given to people by a law or a government. A freedom is the power to act without anyone getting in the way. The Canadian Charter of Rights and Freedoms promises these things. Canadians can meet and talk with whomever they want. They have the right to feel safe. No matter what age, race, or gender people are, all Canadians should be treated fairly.

There are two official languages in Canada: English and French. However, if anyone speaks a different language, they can do so freely. Walking down the street in a major city, a person could hear many different languages being spoken. Canadians can speak in whatever language they want.

Culture is the heart of every nation. Music, books, and movies are all part of a nation's culture. Canadians have the

Montréal, Québec, is Canada's largest French-speaking city.

4

PRIDE TORONTO

Canadians have the freedom to be whoever they want to be. Pride Toronto celebrates that concept with a 10-day event every year. It is one of the largest gay pride festivals in the world. The event celebrates people in the **LGBTQ** community.

freedom to make any kind of art that they like. Canadian culture is as **diverse** as the people living in Canada. Having such diversity creates exciting movies, music, and art. The Government of Canada gives money to support this creativity. Every year, the Canadian Council for the Arts gives $12 million to different artists and groups.

However, **discrimination** still happens in Canada. Discrimination can happen when a person does not receive certain rights and/or freedoms because of how they look or what they believe. The Government of Canada is working to make sure this does not happen. For example, Canada's **Indigenous** Peoples have struggled to be treated fairly for centuries. But in 1982, the **Constitution** of Canada was updated. The Canadian Charter of Rights and Freedoms was added. This update included the **protection** of the rights of Indigenous Peoples. Over the years, the Government of Canada has helped more people enjoy equal rights. The country has come a long way. However, more change is needed.

Thousands of people gather at Pride Toronto every year.

Chapter Two

PERSONAL RIGHTS

The Canadian Constitution contains the values and beliefs that guide the country. Canadians believe in freedom. They understand that no person is above the law. This is called the Rule of Law. No one who serves in government is more important than the people he or she serves. The Charter of Rights and Freedoms was created to make sure government officials would always answer to the people. The Charter protects Canadians. It makes sure people are treated equally. It describes how Canadians are free. Canadians understand they can act, think, and believe whatever they want. They can voice their opinions. They can join groups and organizations. They do not have to worry about being treated badly by people in power. They know that if their freedoms are not being supported they can take action.

> The most important way for Canadians to make sure the Rule of Law is followed is to vote. That way they have a voice in choosing the country's leaders.

Rights and freedoms protect Canadians. For example, every Canadian has the right to life. If someone is sick or hurt, he or she must be taken care of. Hospitals and clinics have doctors and nurses to care for those in need. Canadians have the right to be treated for illness or injury no matter their age, gender, or race.

Canadians also have the right to safety. Anti-bullying laws are in place to protect people from bullies, both in person and online. Children have all of the same rights as adults. Governments have programs in place to protect a child's right to safety.

Living in Canada means all **citizens** have personal rights. These are protected and supported by the Supreme Court of Canada. The Supreme Court reviews the law. It makes sure the Canadian Constitution is being followed. Much of Canada's sense of freedom comes from the government's commitment to every citizen's rights and freedoms.

THE SUPREME COURT

The Supreme Court of Canada is the highest court in the country. It is the last place for rulings and decisions made in court hearings. The Supreme Court serves all Canadians. It does so by deciding legal issues that are important to the public.

The Supreme Court of Canada is located in Ottawa, Ontario.

Chapter Three

FREE TO BE

The rights and freedoms of all Canadians must be valued. Living in Canada means people can believe and say what they want.

In Canada, everyone has the freedom to voice their opinion. People on talk shows and news channels do this every day. Authors write what they want to in books, online, and in newspapers. If a person does not agree with the government, he or she can say so without getting into trouble. As with all rights, this comes with **responsibility**. People have to be careful. No one can say lies or hurtful things about another person.

Canadians are free to practise any religion. **Immigration** brings many different religions

Morning talk shows are a popular outlet for leaders and celebrities to voice their opinions and beliefs.

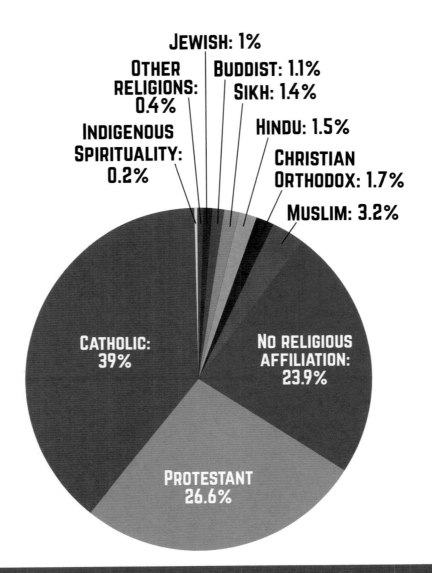

JEWISH: 1%

OTHER RELIGIONS: 0.4%

BUDDIST: 1.1%

SIKH: 1.4%

INDIGENOUS SPIRITUALITY: 0.2%

HINDU: 1.5%

CHRISTIAN ORTHODOX: 1.7%

MUSLIM: 3.2%

CATHOLIC: 39%

NO RELIGIOUS AFFILIATION: 23.9%

PROTESTANT 26.6%

This graph shows the breakdown of religions in Canada.

into Canada. People coming from other countries bring their own religious practises. Protecting religious freedom strengthens the Canadian identity. People in Canada can worship in any way they see fit. No one is told what to believe or how to practise those beliefs.

Many peaceful protests have taken place in Canada. Canadians are free to gather any time they want to voice their opinion.

Religious rights should also be protected at work. People cannot be fired from a job for their beliefs. If they need to take time to pray during the day, that is their right. It should not be held against them. Schools must also protect religious rights. No one should be forced to act in a way that goes against his or her beliefs. If a student wears a head covering, he or she is allowed to do so in school. The student should not be discriminated against. Students do not have to participate in an activity they feel is against their beliefs.

It is every Canadian's right to take part in peaceful meetings. Sometimes people march in large groups to

voice their opinions. Peaceful gatherings are a part of Canada's culture. Canadians have the right to gather together in peace. However, the police can step in if the gathering turns violent. The police will break up a gathering if it is dangerous or it is hurting other people.

Another freedom Canadians enjoy is the right to belong to any group. In Canada, citizens can belong to any organization they choose. This freedom allows people to join Girl Guides, Boy Scouts, athletic teams, and other groups.

Canada is a big country. Another right Canadians have is to travel and live wherever they want to. For example, if someone is born in Ontario, he or she is free to move to another part of the country, such as British Columbia. Any Canadian can earn a living in any province they choose. Citizens are free to leave Canada, as well.

Canadians have a lot of freedoms. With these freedoms comes the opportunity to help others, like this Scouts Canada group did with their efforts to help the environment.

Chapter Four

A DIVERSE NATION

A basic right of all Canadians is the right to be treated equally under the law. Every citizen is considered equal no matter his or her background or beliefs. This is important because of Canada's diversity. Canada is a nation of immigrants. Over the years, people have moved to Canada from all over the world. But diversity is more than just where a person comes from or what a person looks like. Diversity in Canada includes gender, religion, abilities, and language.

Indigenous Peoples include First Nations, Métis, and Inuit. They have a special place in Canada. They were here first, before any settlers arrived. Canada has not always treated Indigenous Peoples fairly.

Canada's Indigenous Peoples are an important part of the country's identity.

RECONCILIATION CANADA

Reconciliation Canada has a mission to build strong, healthy relationships between Indigenous Peoples and all Canadians. They started an idea for Indigenous Peoples and other Canadians to walk 4 kilometres together and discuss a better future every year. More than 70,000 people came out in downtown Vancouver, British Columbia, to participate in 2013.

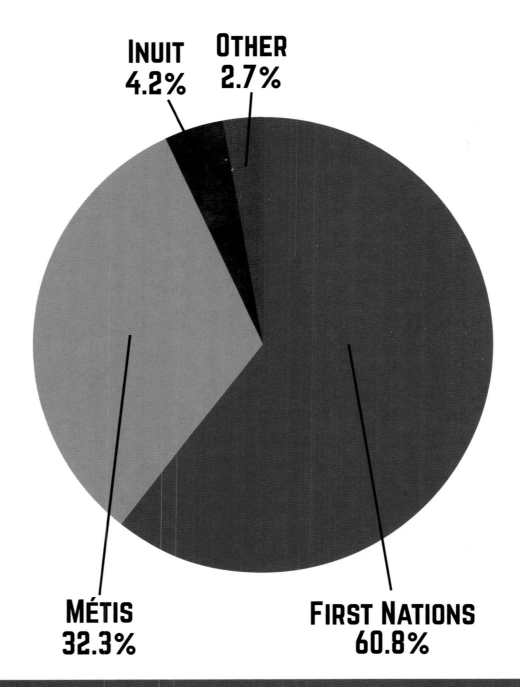

INUIT
4.2%

OTHER
2.7%

MÉTIS
32.3%

FIRST NATIONS
60.8%

This chart shows the breakdown of Indigenous Peoples in Canada as of 2011.

They have not always been given the same rights and freedoms as other citizens. The Government of Canada told them how to act. It would not let Indigenous Peoples wear traditional clothing. They were told what to believe. Their children were taken and sent to **residential schools**. This was a dark time in Canadian history. The Government of Canada has made efforts to fix this. The Government is working on its communication with Indigenous Peoples. It started by recognizing their customs and beliefs. The Government is working to change its relationship with Indigenous Peoples. It sees the mistakes of the past and wants a brighter future. But there still is a long way to go.

INQUIRY QUESTION

How do immigrants make Canada a stronger country and a better place to live?

Canada celebrates its heritage and diversity. The country is always working to protect and increase the freedom of its people. For example, Canada is working to increase Internet access across the country. The Internet is an important tool for sharing and receiving information. People without access to reliable Internet have less freedom to share and receive information than those who do have access.

GLOSSARY

CITIZENS
members of a community or country

CONSTITUTION
a set of rules that guides a country

CULTURE
ways of life, ideas, or traditions

DISCRIMINATION
unfair behaviour toward someone because of their age, race, gender, or religion

DIVERSE
when there are many kinds of something; for example, a society is diverse if it includes people from different countries

IMMIGRATION
when people come to a foreign country to live

INDIGENOUS
naturally existing or occurring in a place rather than arriving from another place

LGBTQ
an acronym that stands for lesbian, gay, bisexual, transgender, and queer

PROTECTION
the act of defending or looking after something or someone

RESIDENTIAL SCHOOLS
schools that Indigenous children were forced to attend by the Government of Canada where they lost their sense of tradition and culture

RESPONSIBILITY
a duty

TO LEARN MORE

BOOKS

Hacker, Carlotta. *The Kids Book of Canadian History*. Toronto, ON: Kids Can Press, 2009.

Rodger, Ellen. *How Does the Canadian Government Work?* St. Catharines, ON: Crabtree Publishing Company, 2013.

Ruurs, Margriet. *Stepping Stones: A Refugee Family's Journey*. Victoria, BC: Orca Book Publishers, 2016.

WEBSITES

CANADA'S HISTORY FOR KIDS
http://kids.canadashistory.ca/Kids/Home.aspx

JOHN HUMPHREY CENTRE: YOUTH GUIDE TO THE CANADIAN CHARTER OF RIGHTS AND FREEDOMS
http://www.bestlibrary.org/ss11/files/charterguide.pdf

NELSON: WHY ARE CANADA'S RIGHTS AND FREEDOMS IMPORTANT?
http://www.nelson.com/albertasocialstudies/productinfo/gr6_9/docs/abss6ch5.pdf

INDEX

ABOUT THE AUTHOR

Joy Kita is a proud Canadian citizen. She lives in Ontario and works as a freelance writer. She is the author of the Fable Nation series for kids. She is married and has four children.